Feed The "Write" Piggy Bank

*A Writer's Mini-Wisdom Guide
For Making Leveraged & Lucrative
Career Decisions*

Alicia "WATERS"

Copyright © 2014 Alicia "WATERS"

All rights reserved. Except for use in the case of brief quotations embodied in critical articles and reviews, the reproduction or utilization of this work in whole or part in any form by any electronic, digital, mechanical or other means, now known or hereafter invented, including xerography, photocopying, scanning, recording, or any information storage or retrieval system, is forbidden without prior written permission of the author and publisher.

The scanning, uploading, and distribution of this book via the Internet or via any other means without permission of the publisher and author is illegal and punishable by law. Purchase only authorized versions of this book and do not participate in or encourage electronic piracy of copyrighted materials. Your support of the author's rights is appreciated.

Names, characters, places, and incidents are based on the author's own personal experience therefore names of persons and entities remain unnamed to protect the integrity of the story and the privacy of those involved. Any group or organization listed is for informational purposes only and does not imply endorsement or support of their activities or organization.

For ordering, booking, permission, or questions, contact the author.

www.anwempires@gmail.com

www.amazon.com/author/alicianwaters

ISBN-13:978-1494981013

ISBN-10:1494981017

Printed in the United States of America by Create Space

Feed The "Write" Piggy Bank

Dedication & Acknowledgment

This book is a general dedication to all writers who are on the journey of achieving their highest levels of potential, making an impact on others, while creating the wealthy lifestyles that they deserve.

I give thanks and acknowledgments to God and all who have assisted and/or inspired me on my writing journey.

Feed The "Write" Piggy Bank

Table of Contents

Introduction

Do You Do The "Write" Thing?

Choosing My "Write" Way to Go & Grow

Does It Add Up to the "Write" Amount?

How to Cure Piggy Bank Starvation Syndrome for Writers

Always Think Bigger Than the Published Book

Don't Know What to Do? Just Blog

Conscious Intentional Blogging for Business

Increase Your Income Using Facebook Fan Pages as Mini Blogs

Start Your Mini Publishing Empire Through Createspace

Conclusion

Introduction

In the areas of time, value and money, avid writers often sell themselves short. In turn, this results in a lack of effectively leveraging time, not valuing themselves along with earning either a little to no money at all for their efforts.

Time, value and money truly deserve to be respected and honored if writers desire to see more abundance flow into their lives. Often, when any of these areas are abused as it relates to the work that we do, the question of worthiness needs to be addressed.

Examining your worth concerning every area of life is critical. Doing an honest inventory to assess how you are respecting time, value and money will provide a measurable tracking system of evaluating your current levels of worthiness.

If we desire to see greater opportunities and manifestations flow into our lives with our writing careers, then we must begin to honor and value ourselves especially in the areas of time and money. It's time for writers to stop selling themselves short in order to achieve the career success in which they desire.

Feed The "Write" Piggy Bank

Feed The "Write" Piggy Bank

Making daily decisions about best wisdom practices can be challenging at times, especially if so much of our internal and external resources have been spent trying to accomplish our goals. *Feed The "Write" Piggy Bank,* is a mini handbook with concepts that aid and assist avid writers with aligning their efforts in making l*everaged and lucrative career decisions.*

Do You Do the "Write" Thing?

I came across a question once on the Facebook fan page of million-dollar marketing coach, Kendall Summerhawk, where she asked the question; Are you more worried about doing things right, or doing the right things? This is a question I ask myself often, in fact almost every other day when it comes to my writing endeavors. Trying to figure out which right is right for writing can be a bit challenging at times.

I've chosen to rephrase this question by asking myself; Am I writing right/correctly from a grammatical standpoint or am I writing the right type of content? I believe that there is a divine balance in having the ability to operate from both ends of the spectrum when necessary. The catch is trying to figure out which right is right at the right time for the who, what when and how to write.

In the children's show Barney, there is a character named Baby Bop who sang a song once called, What Should I Do?

Chorus: What should I do? What should I do? What should I do, when I don't know what I should do?

So, what should you do? Which write is right? I've chosen to adopt a "No Wrong Way to Write," approach by choosing what love would have me to write. The only wrong thing to do is to not write at all.

I simply move out of stagnation, make my writing decisions, make them right for me and my target audience. There is no wrong way because love always chooses the right way and allows us to course correct along the way. Therefore, I can always write the right things.

Choosing My Write Way to Go & Grow

As a multi-industries journalist, I have to always be very mindful of how I'm crafting my writing ventures. My styles and workflow for writing are probably very different from most writers because I provide content for diverse industries that individually have very different needs. For this reason, I have to create my own writing agenda my way.

Writing my way is all about choosing the divine right/write ways to go and grow my business, impact my audience, as well as advance my personal and professional life.

Feed The "Write" Piggy Bank

Before I began to intuitively co-create the writing experiences that I desire, I mindfully examine arising opportunities, my current goals and financial obligations to determine which direction I desire to take.

Does It Add Up to the "Write" Amount?

When it comes to honoring my total worth as a writer, I have to use my *"Triple L"* alignment assessment that I created for holistic balance. This alignment assessment stands for, Liberating, Leveraging & Lucrative. This helps me to determine what clients or assignments for a particular industry that will I take on.

I make it a practice of consciously choosing the right writing projects, aligned creative contributors, and publishing options. I intentionally position my energy to only get involved with endeavors that are going to be for the highest and best good for both myself and the other party.

I've learned that time, energy and money are three of the most commonly abused resources through unconscious mismanagement. Every day individuals are making unaligned choices that cost them royally in those three areas.

Experiences have taught me to challenge myself everyday by taking an inventory of how I spend my time, energy and resources to evaluate if my activities are in *"Triple L"* alignment.

Feed The "Write" Piggy Bank

In some of my trainings intensives for avid writers or for clients, I often encourage them to create what I call, nothing less than twin projects. This involves taking one project and making it into many things. This makes the *"Triple L"* formula work like magic.

To avoid making unwise career moves when it comes to your writing and publishing endeavors, begin to better examine if the opportunities or efforts are adding up to the "Write" amount for what you desire or require in order to be "*Triple L*" aligned.

How to Cure Piggy Bank Starvation Syndrome for Writers

Often, writers bank accounts are under-nourished because they've spent too much time feeding the wrong piggy bank by engaging in certain writing endeavors or joint ventures that don't pay off well in the long run.

Not following intuitive leads when it comes to your writing careers can put you in compromising situations that waste your time, resources and energy.

This results in distractions from a lack of vision that keeps most from choosing those opportunities that could be more leveraged and lucrative. It's time to stop starving your piggy bank.

Feed The "Write" Piggy Bank

It's time for authors and writers to move beyond the feast or famine syndrome, by learning how to effectively feed a malnutrition bank account that has been starving from a lack of purposeful profits.

The two common cures are combining intuition and alignment when it comes to your writing efforts.

Practicing intuitive alignment is a life saver for assisting authors with eliminating any unaligned writing assignments that distract them from connecting with the more aligned opportunity that could bring more wealth and freedom into their experience.

Always Think Bigger Than the Published Book

Often, most authors write a book or a series of books and still don't see their desired results from their book sales. They also get frustrated by not achieving the impact that they wanted to make through reaching many.

Limitations of only thinking in a linear process for the book itself is always a stumbling block from the start. Authors should always think bigger than the book before writing it. Most, only think of writing the book, becoming published, having book signings and sales.

Written masterpieces desire to become programs, home studies, certification programs or even films and/or radio productions. The possibilities are endless. You can create workshops/seminars and so much more.

Feed The "Write" Piggy Bank

One chapter from your book could potentially springboard into something bigger than the book itself. Your book could launch a new business career or mini-service.

I've learned from my first publishing experience when I saw my first book project be transformed into several things until that particular book had to be revised and broken down into other projects. People were much more attracted to the other offerings that sprung from the book that the book itself was no longer the big thing.

Also, authors often forget to remember that people desire to buy into them as a person first and then their books and everything else that they offer will become automatic. Again, it is always bigger than the book.

Don't Know What to Do? Just Blog

Blogging is one of the fastest growing and lucrative industries for writers of all kinds to get their messages out into the world. Blogging is very important and the writing process provides a greater sense of awareness for personal and professional evolution than most people realize.

I am an avid blogger and at times blogging has really and truly been my saving grace when I don't know which direction I should take when it comes to reaching my goals. Every time I find myself beginning to get overly concerned about my forward movement, a small voice always says, just write, just write, just blog.

Feed The "Write" Piggy Bank

I like the "Keep Calm," slogans, especially as it relates to blogging. For me blogging is not just about reaching my target audience or making money, it is also very therapeutic and healing. As a writer, I've known for quite a while that writing, in general, is therapeutic, yet blogging takes on a higher level of feeling productive, purposeful and prosperous.

There is something about blogging that makes you feel like you are empowering the world at large while often releasing some of your brilliance and personal and professional transparency as an online journal.

Blogging is so important because you never know what great idea might be sparked through your writings or who might come across your blog and have their lives changed. If you change their life, then you've changed your life as well. So, in moments when you begin to feel all over the place or don't know what to do, just keep calm and blog on.

Conscious Intentional Blogging for Business

As you've heard me mention that blogging is very important not just for reaching your target audience or making money, but also because it can be therapeutic.

Yet, there comes a time where you must align your blogging with pure intentionality as it relates to your business endeavors.

Feed The "Write" Piggy Bank

Though I can be great at being moved to do some freestyle blogging, however, I certainly have to be very intentional about my blogging as it relates to achieving my business goals. I have to bring a higher level of consciousness to what I'm engaged in.

Blogging for business is not just about blogging to try to gain more clients or make sales with one of your amazing products, it's also about creating a conscious community with others who share similar expertise or interest. People desire to gain knowledge from you or even possibly see how you both can work together to empower more people and make it lucrative for both parties while adding value to the world.

I believe in establishing what I call, conscious business transparency as it relates to blogging for income, creating opportunities and/or connections. Everyone has to make a living and deserves to achieve their highest levels of success.

Increase Your Income Using Facebook Fan-Pages as Mini Blogs

Blogging has become one of the top money making revenue streams that are being used by several and not just avid writers. There are many ways to market your blogs, yet most writers are leaving a lot of money on the table by not using their Facebook fan pages effectively by allowing them to serve as mini-blogs.

Posting without conscious intention leaves the door wide open for creating the vibration of just having another fan page that just looks like it's just a posting ground of continuous content with no real direction.

Creating intentionally with all of your writing endeavors is what separates true writers' and authors' content from something that is being posted as just another fan page status.

Making connections, advertising products, and services in a nonlinear way is another reason why Facebook fan pages are a great medium to use as mini-blogs. The income opportunities are limitless even without using the paid ads when you market in this manner.

Fan pages as mini-blogs can help to leverage time efficiently by using the timers features to set up brief posts to go out when you desire. Your page can be in concert with your main blog or even use the page as a lead into your main blog. You can also offer your Facebook followers (not necessarily friend connections) special promotions or create mini-events especially for them.

There is no one formula for fan page success, however, discovering how to creatively use it as a blog will have your special touch of genius. The goal is to consider using it as another writing platform to increase your impact and income.

Feed The "Write" Piggy Bank

Start Your Mini Publishing Empire Through Createspace

For anyone who is interested in starting their own publishing company in the future, Createspace is a great platform to begin building your brand and learning the ends and outs of self-publishing with excellence.

Createspace, an Amazon company, has so many options to serve first-time authors and avid writers that allow them to publish the way they desire and as often as possible.

They provide a free ISBN and an option that allows you to include your own logo as the publisher. This is an awesome way to begin branding your publications for your future publishing company.

The great news is that there is no cost to publish, they supply free distribution channels and print on demand for your customers.

I use Createspace as my mini-lead-in of my forth-coming publication platform that will eventually serve as a publishing company. I'm using my own company logo on certain selections of my books to establish my brand and gain exposure as I'm building my own empire.

I love being able to be in control of my publishing endeavors and having the luxury of using a platform like www.createspace.com. Their turnaround time for reviewing your manuscript to meet the standard requirements is phenomenal. After your book is approved by you, then it immediately goes up for sale on your selected distribution channels.

Feed The "Write" Piggy Bank

Conclusion

There is no better time than now to begin creating a new reality for you and your family. Now more than ever writers are desiring to live from a place of serving from their passions while enjoying a sizable income through solo-entrepreneurship.

What greater way to provide inspiration and learning than writing publications of many forms. This gives you an opportunity to create works and services that will change lives. The *"Time Is Now"* to go after your dreams and you can do this in shorter time frames with grace and ease using the insights from this book.

Whether you're a new writer, already published or a current business owner, just know that your current level is more than enough for the moment to change someone's life. At some point or another, you might reach a point in your writing journey where it seems like you've been doing all that you can when it comes to being a better writer, sell more books or even making a bigger impact without seeing measurable results.

It's at those times where you dig deep within and say "I AM Enough." So, the next time you feel like you are not enough or someone else makes you feel like you're not enough, just remember that you are enough. You get to choose how you will show up in your creativity as a writer by embracing your simple truth that you are more than enough for your current audience.

Feed The "Write" Piggy Bank

Reflections & Actions
(Record reflections from the reading to create a plan)

Feed The "Write" Piggy Bank

More Notes:

Feed The "Write" Piggy Bank

Reflections & Actions
(Record reflections from the reading to create a plan)

Feed The "Write" Piggy Bank

More Notes:

Feed The "Write" Piggy Bank

Reflections & Actions
(Record reflections from the reading to create a plan)

Feed The "Write" Piggy Bank

More Notes:

Feed The "Write" Piggy Bank

Reflections & Actions
(Record reflections from the reading to create a plan)

Feed The "Write" Piggy Bank

More Notes:

Feed The "Write" Piggy Bank

Reflections & Actions
(Record reflections from the reading to create a plan)

Feed The "Write" Piggy Bank

More Notes:

Feed The "Write" Piggy Bank

Reflections & Actions
(Record reflections from the reading to create a plan)

Feed The "Write" Piggy Bank

More Notes:

Feed The "Write" Piggy Bank

Other Related Books
Feed the Right Piggy Bank
This Little Piggy Went Marketing
I Like Frog Legs & Ham
Fattening Your Piggy Bank
Profitable Aha Moments
Creating Profitable Piggy Banks

Feed The "Write" Piggy Bank

For More Resources:

Visit:

www.profitablepiggybankspower.blogspot.com

www.amazon.com/author/alicianwaters

Or

To Book the Author

For Speaking Engagements

Email: www.anwempires@gmail.com

If you enjoyed this resource, please consider writing a review on Amazon.com.

Thanks & Blessings!

Feed The "Write" Piggy Bank

www.ingramcontent.com/pod-product-compliance
Lightning Source LLC
Chambersburg PA
CBHW070731180526
45167CB00004B/1708